The Pen Is The Most Powerful Weapon

I0433623

JyJuan Brock

Written by JyJuan Brock

Published by Writers Block Publishing LLC

www.writersblockpublishingllc.com

The Pen Is The Most Powerful Weapon

The Pen Is the Most Powerful Weapon

The Power of the Pen gave me the opportunity to express my emotion, and a therapeutic tool for healing. Once I began to address my issues mentally, physically, and spiritually. Many people ask me how did I get the topics to express myself, my respond is God placed the topics in my heart. My life journey has allowed me to be able to put my feelings on paper so I can be set free. My mom use to say the truth will set you free; God looks at your heart not your faults. Now I'm back in the Criminal Justice System due to unresolved issues.

All my life I looked for acceptance and love through people, rather it was negative or positive. I always knew something was wrong but never had the courage to address the traumas that haunted me all my life.

The emotional and spiritual crisis we talk, but never address is mental health. Mental Health is real, and most men don't address this because there is a stigma attached to it.

Mental Health is also very serious. It is vital that we understand that mental health wears many masks. On the outside, it might appear as if nothing is going on, but deep down you're dying on the inside.

Each one of my poems has help me to be set free from the bondage of pain, low self-worth, loneness, acceptance, validation, fear, rejection, abandonment, and through my poetry I now have acceptance and power over my own life. Sometimes God can make a negative situation be a positive outcome and save my life. Today physically, my body is in prison but I refuse to allow it to corrupt my
mind. My pen gives me the

JyJuan Brock

ability to freely express my inner feeling when there was a time I kept it hidden. If I was able to speak how I write I can be a motivation speaker and help those who struggle from the enemy within, we all live with.

The Pen Is The Most Powerful Weapon

The Pen is Mightier Than The Sword

In more ways than one, the pen is way mightier than the sword.
It's a mean of self-expression when unable to vocalize your words.

Making it easier to understand different culture and religion
How would we know our history if there was no one to document it?

Going way back before in time, Judges, presidents politician and lawyers.
Use the pen to sign off on amendments and sentencing orders.

The declaration that we live by, the abolishment of slavery
The end of racial segregation throughout the black and white communities,
The pen ended it all, but could also cause a war
It was used to change the laws in the state and federal reforms.

The times keep changing but so should the laws
Writing proposals for grants, and programs to aid in criminal justice.

Drug reforms and rehabilitation to halt the revolving cycle
The Torah, the Quran, and even the Holy Bible
All tell a story that we wouldn't know if there wasn't a pen to write it.

Weapons never fully ended war, take your time and think about that?

JyJuan Brock

It was always by a document in the form of a treaty,
Where two signs on the dotted line because they came to an agreement.

The change in equality allowing women to vote
All came from a single stroke.
Pencil pushers sitting back, jotting down every note
Intrigued by the information given
From my mental picture that I wrote.

Affirmation: Psalms 45:1: My heart overflows with a good theme: I address my verses to the King: My tongue is the pen of a ready writer.

The Pen Is The Most Powerful Weapon

Eight Twenty- Two

I sealed my fate from my mistakes;
I'll have to live with for the rest of my life.
Hard to tell behind a vacant shell,
All the hurt that stuck inside.
By circumstances, this became one of the hardest moments
That I dealt with in my life,
Not knowing how to fix it, or how to make it right.

Face to face with my worst fears,
While battling all of my demons.
Comprehending from experience,
That everything happens for a reason.

Woke up feeling a little tense,
My spirit was uneasy,
Got my daughter dressed,
She ate her breakfast in front of my T.V.

Once I was mentally together,
Said a silent prayer prior to leaving
I in no way knew this would be the final time that I could embrace my baby.

At least that was the plan,
But it didn't go as attended.
Dropped her off to school, she acted as if she knew today would be the last time she'd see me.

JyJuan Brock

Heart full of pain, disappointment, and regrets
It's like my princess sensed that something was wrong
because she didn't want me to leave.
This is the day that I will never forget

Uncertain of my next move,
This something that I can now admit.
By understand the options,
My selections grew slimmer by the minute.
My attentions were never bad,
Though my actions told a story that was different.

Walked to my lawyers office, but he was in a meeting
One of his associates was preparing my case for today's
court proceedings.
The plan was to postpone, for obvious reasons
As of yet I knew that I didn't have a warrant
I was still on probations; my plan was to attempt to beat it.

Had to prepare myself mentally,
For what was next to come
This would be the third continuance,
Due to lack of evidence.

The victim wasn't showing up,
That much was pretty obvious
He would then, ask for a dismissal if not another continuance.

My lawyer had a temperament of confidence and arrogance,
This seemed to slightly calm my nerves,

The Pen Is The Most Powerful Weapon

But heightened my other senses.
He ensured me that I was coming home,
And I would make myself sick from worrying
My perception of his methods,
Was to divert the truth of what was really happening.
I met my mother at my job and we walked as one to my preliminary hearing.

Making idle conversation about getting my life together.
One of the longest walk either of us ever had to endeavor.
Though wasn't planned,
We both managed to wear the same color.
Hoping to be in and out
So we could spend her birthday together.

Having a birthday brunch, and later treating her to dinner
This is a day that I never forget.
Heart full of pain, disappointment, and regrets
Uncertain of my next move,
This is something that I now admit.

My plan was to talk her to lunch, then later to dinner.
It was my mom's birthday 8/22.
She sensed something was wrong
But was waiting for me to admit that.
We share a special bond and she felt what I was feeling.
 A mother intuition constantly goes beyond the normal limits.

JyJuan Brock

I gave her a list just in case she ever had to use it
Filled with phone number and amounts of specific people
who still owe me.
First, I had to sign in and wait for my lawyer to arrive
As we walked into the court room
My anxiety immediately began to climb.
The judge slowly entered from his chambers;
The sheriff gave specific instructions for everyone to turn
Their phones off while yelling: "To All Rise!!!"

Court was now in session;
He wore his gown and held his gavel
At this point, everything started moving as smoothly as scheduled
However, when he pronounce my name;
My life forever change.

Mother's breathing became unsettled,
And her actions were irate. The judge
called me to his bench,
For me to sign my postponement.

Although I didn't know it,
I had a warrant for probation.
As I began to walk away,
A sheriff grabbed me and called my name.
A single tear ran down my mother's face,
And pierced my heart in more ways than one.

Couldn't imagine
Letting my mom down wasn't even a fraction.
Because literally turned her special day into a disaster

The Pen Is The Most Powerful Weapon

By far the worst birthday gift that any mother could imagine.

Two walked in, but she became the solitary on standing
With hurt and compassion.
Seeing her first born being cuffed and arrested.
Overwhelm and feeling helpless,
Since there was no means for her to help me
Nevertheless, she remained in my corner, and continued to be supportive.

The realist must have raised her, you could tell by how my momma grew up.

Affirmation: Romans 13:1; Let every person be subject to the governing authorities. For there is no authority except from God, and those that exist have been instituted by God.

JyJuan Brock

Life Of An Inmate

Becoming acclimated to insanity conditions
Stripped completely naked,
Degraded and desecrated,
Everything that differentiates us as a human being swept completely away.
Constitutional rights taken, before ever having your judgement day.

Throughout the intake process, your identities replaced
Documenting your height, tattoos, eye color and your weight.
Collecting every piece of information placing it inside a data base.
Classified based on prior criminal history, and the immediate offense.

Some guards will treat you like an animal As
if we are scum under their shoes.
Hiding behind a badge, like they have a point to prove.
Respect is everything, though we have nothing to lose Just because we are in jail, that doesn't make us any less equal.

Once processing is complete, you will be given a specified color of scrubs.
To determine your work assignment or housing unit, before you make it to a pod.
There are four different stages people adhere while imprison,
Denial, sadness, anger, and acceptance.

The Pen Is The Most Powerful Weapon

When assigned to a specific block, become familiarized of your surroundings.
Scare tactics used often, to weed out the weakest target
Wolves searching for prey, planning on extortion.

Rule number one, don't ask, and don't borrow
Always be the one to lead, never be the man to follow
All you have in prison is your word don't brand yourself as a liar.
Majority come to jail, allegedly pursuing a dollar and a dream.

Burning every bridge along the way, to justify their means
Deceit, is just another word for manipulations.
Watch out for ones trying to jump on people's cases.
The loudest in the room is only thriving for attention.
No matter where you go there will exist one in attendance.

Rule number two, stay faraway from those types of people
Relationships become non-existent,
Stressing over women that's only playing with your feelings.
Stress boxing on the phone, constantly going back and forth arguing.
Random cell searching, trying to case you up for anything
Monitored phone calls and visits record anything slightly incriminating.

JyJuan Brock

Making copies of your photos and mail,
Ensuring no contraband or different of drugs contaminated your property
Little to no room for privacy, you lost the privilege during processing.

Rule number three, always mind your own business
Institutional predators lie in wait searching for their next
Vic Those are the ones that's patiently trying to catch,

Trying to bring a straight man into the darkest depths
Once you crossover that line, there is no coming back.
Homosexuals alongside straight men forced to coexist
Predators go for individuals that appear to be the softest.
Inmates might have seen it, but nobody intervenes.

Gambling becomes an issue because everybody's wealth isn't on the wood
Derogatory statements turn into arguments
Claiming a person is snitching even with lack of evidence
All since an individual doesn't like you, it's never just a coincidence.

Same ones pointing the fingers would sell out the own mother and friends just to keep the focus off of them
Don't ever borrow anything from anyone
Rats are lowest of the low in the prison hierarchy Guilt by association is all they really need.

The Pen Is The Most Powerful Weapon

Avoid unnecessary conflict by staying in our lane.
All alone with just your thoughts, nothing but idle time on
our hands.
Some study to become a better criminal
Other proclaim their life to God claiming their life has changed.

Why lie to self, the circumstances are still the same
Prison becomes a revolving door, No intentions on
ever making amends.
Commissary prices outrageous, a single soup is $1.05

Atrocious provisions fed is barely enough to survive
Jail indeed, makes individuals use their creativity
More out of necessity due to feeding and living
inadequacies.

Certain inhabitants you may encounter
Often becomes closer than equal family
Their loyalty superseded their underlying ways of old friends
and relatives.

We are all in the same boat, though circumstances are different
Other than death, jail is the lowest form of living

Hebrew: 13:3; Remember them that are in bonds, and bounds with them, (and) them which sugger adversity, as being yourself also in the body

JyJuan Brock

Fully Committed

Excuse me for talking excessively, faltering over my words
Honesty is the best policy; can you handle the truth?
Is there a quiet place to talk, where you and I can be alone?
Without holding anything against me for the one weakness
I've exposed.

For a long time, I've waited for the chance to give another soul
my heart.
Trust has already been proven, loyalty ranked at number one.
Stepping right in, before I realized how profound we really were.
A captivating link; when two opposite can magnetize as one.
Committed to one another, my heart is now within your grasp.
Visualizing our potential future while leaving behind the past.

Feeling of love and empathy, releasing negative energy
The only place that we've predestined to go, is whatever
place that we decide to be.
Whatever our mind can conceive and believe, it can also
achieve. It doesn't matter how slow we move as long as
we don't ever stop.

The real question isn't who is going to let us;
 Nevertheless, who is going to deter us from climbing all the
way to the top?
Our lives commence to end we become unvoiced about issues
that truly matter.

The Pen Is The Most Powerful Weapon

Try not to apply pressure; certain events in life are destined
Instant chemical reaction once two liquids are ingested
A full commitment meant to last for life, with love and devotion invested.

Affirmation: Psalms 37.5 Commit thy way unto the Lord trust also in him and he shall bring it to pass.

Women's Intuition

From birth they were born with a sixth sense that all females have.
Their intuition like a super power they encompass over men.
Women are the most complicated creatures, and the hardest to understand.

Anticipating actions before it happens, while men are unaware of why they're mad.
Everyone has heard of mother's intuition ten days ahead?
Women been had this ability way before they ever had any children.

Have you ever heard the saying,
You got to wake up ten days ahead?
To ever pull a smooth one over or under a woman's head
They see what we don't see and hear what we don't hear.

Listening to every word, while analyzing the person tone
They know who you are talking to before you even get off the phone.

Females create time to plot and investigate
Weeding out the truths, while making sure there's nothing you can fabricate.

The master of illusion and the queen in disguise,
Special agent 007, what she wants to identify she will find.
Digging yourself into a ditch before you even realize
Once the target is set, she'll slowly claim her prize.

The Pen Is The Most Powerful Weapon

Her intuition is her secret weapon what works every time.

She knows when a person has bad intent,
Before you wink an eye.
Her instinct keeps you fully alert with her extra set of eyes.

Affirmation: Ephesians 6:2 Honor your father and your mother that your days may be long that the Lord your giving you.

JyJuan Brock

Save Me

Fake people you can't get caught up in your feeling with
Warning signs will show you exactly who you're dealing with.
Wishing I could turn the hands of time to days when my mind
and body was celibate.

Purity, and change the course of the life I've inherit,
Focus on yourself, never too much on the opposite Being
save from political issues, people and public ignorance.

From the mister knows it all that carries a tone of arrogance
Save me from facial profiling and becoming a threat to my
environment.
Maturity and humility, allows you to admit that you're ready
for saving.

Gun fully loaded, extended magazine, no safety
One in the chamber, as if my whole existence is in
jeopardy.
Accidental discharge, by slander got in the way
Pure awareness for common sense, insures that the past will never
change.

The Pen Is The Most Powerful Weapon

I don't want to block my blessings, and keep me from being saved.
Living life full of secrets and regrets, the majority end up talking to the grave.
Save Me.

Affirmation: Psalms 69: 1 God save me. My troubles are like a flood. I'm up to my neck.

JyJuan Brock

How can I love until I love me?

It's only after we've stepped outside of our comfort zone, we will then commence to change.
How can you truly love another soul, if you still have selfish ways?
Some roads you have to walk alone, with no means to navigate.
Using stars as a compass hopeful to one day find a mean to escape.

Learn to love self first, before choosing your love away
You will always have yourself, forever and a day.
True love will shine through the thickest clouds as the storm begins to fade.

No one can help you grow in life better than you can
Find out who you truly are, and then you'll understand
You have to love thyself before times invested in another person.
Your body maybe yearning, but you don't have to take action on it.
Choose to focus your time and energy on people whom inspire you.

Pay close attention since the ones you believe you love might be the demise of you.
We are who we pretend,
Therefore, we must be careful who we pretend to be
Can become your own best friend or your own worst enemy.

The Pen Is The Most Powerful Weapon

What's meant will always find a way
Quitting last forever, but fighting is a temporary pain.
To love and loss will guarantee that one day you'll discover love again.

Be certain that there only focus isn't for a monetary gain
If your morals aren't matching up, and values aren't the same.
Re-evaluate the circumstances, because something has to change.

Every choice we decide to make us, so tread lightly and choose wisely
Educated on what not to do for fear that the next time will happen more precisely
More than livelihood on the line, you can't get a receipt for any loss of time.
Remember, you will not get a refund for days wasted in your life.

The human heart connects directly to the brain.
This can fool a person, making them temporarily insane.
When one door of happiness closes, another soon will open
If we gaze way to long at the closing door, we won't see the one that opened for us.

Making a mental thought because that's a war we need to beat.
The battles that really count are the ones that make you think.

JyJuan Brock

Evaluating our flaws, while searching for the weakest links
The struggles we have inside ourselves are hard for anyone to see.
Life has endless opportunities
Start one step at a time Until
the journey is complete.

The Pen Is The Most Powerful Weapon

Broken

Emotionally, we've on occasion worked a full day in one hour
Weighted by responsibilities, that leaves us mentally and
physically exhausted.

Broken- shattered, to reduce into small fragments.
Blood pressure rises, heart beat racing, Time still
ticking slowly running out of patience, Getting
harder to stand due to lack of foundation.

Burned, stabbed, bullet wounds, abrasions
Life abreacted, I'm just trying to maintain it. Torn,
broken, no reason to deny it.
Flat lined on a stretcher, one breathe away from dying.

The words of the reckless, pieces but heart with a jagged sword.
The tongue of the wise; won't be easily ignored
Healing is a process, many have endured. Hurt
people, hurt people because they too, have been
broken.
Seconds, at a standstill, spirit become frozen

The way that we are treated; should be looked at as an example.
Each person, should be tested upon their own action
To observe the approach, and to see their individuals
reaction.

JyJuan Brock

To understand how if felt, facing similar circumstances
Life of rejection can be a hard pill to process
Easy to glue together an object when it's broken,
You cannot apply glue to restore another person.

Anyone who claims to be in the light, while still hurting others
Will continue to block blessing and remain in the darkness
Many waters could never quench the hurt of being broken

Affirmation: Isaiah 43:2 Even when times are rough and you are in deep waters, leading and guiding you through your worst

The Pen Is The Most Powerful Weapon

All or Nothing

Too many people don't live their dreams, because they are still living in fear.
Afraid to make a change, while floodgates hold back hidden tears.
You may be mad if you take a loss, but you'll be a fool not try
Who will you become, when life changes at a blink of an eye?

Information is an investment, and is a tribute from the wise
Soak up as much, just like a sponge, and embrace it with your life.

Your dispositions not defined by the actions that you take
But how a person responds in the shadows of their wake.
Pay attention to surroundings, when you have so much as stake.

When you let go of who you think you are, you'll be the person that you might be.
An enticement into another's world, could become an instant tragedy.
What has been will one day be again, and what has been done will be done again.

Failing to understand the consequences of being held under contempt.

No one can make you feel dumb, without your consent
There's a big difference between common sense and plain old ignorance.

JyJuan Brock

Don't become a product of your circumstances, but a product of your own decisions.
Play close attention to your senses when instincts begin to kick in.
What makes a person any different than the next in the same position?

An individual who never made a mistake, in no way tried anything new.
Ending in the same situations because they had a point to prove.
It's never too late, to be what you might have always been
Falling seven times, still you get right back up again

Always use precaution with the people you're dealing with
Disguised as an ally to seize all of your hustler's benefits
You won't ever spot them coming because you brought them into the mix.

So how can you fight a war, you never exists.

The Pen Is The Most Powerful Weapon

In the Darkest Hours

Everyone has inner beauty, not everyone can see
In our darkest hour, fear leads to vulnerability
Dig deep to find your courage, survival is a necessity
Follow around by dark rain clouds, floating directly over me.

When it rains, then it pours, releasing the floodgates into the streets.
Watch out! Be on your guard for many different types of greed.
Open your eyes, lying with dogs could lead to catching fleas.

Keep your eyes open, play close attention to your dreams.
The knowledge that I wish to gain is one that defines
What's the real difference between living and existence?
Life isn't determined by abundance of possessions

However, the significance of creating bonds, while making lasting impressions.
It is very crucial to dot each and every I, while crossing every T.
Death is the destiny of every human being.

The living should take this to heart, because there is no days guaranteed.
The date of birth and the date of death are the only ones of certainty.

JyJuan Brock

Looking through the glass of life, as the grains of sand slowly depletes.
The only person we are destined to become, is the person that we decide to be.
I often ask this question, is this life for me?

Affirmation: Psalms 18:6 Far of my distress I called the Lord; the Lord answered me and set me free. The Lord is on my side. I will not fear. What can a Man do to me?

The Pen Is The Most Powerful Weapon

All Alone Trapped

Walking aimless down the stairs
While the dopamine invades the brain
My body is switching gears.
I completely lost my self
Mind starting running scared.

It's sometimes hard to face my fears.
 I stay mentally aware.
Pigment of my flesh began to fade.
As I slowly disappeared.

Objects in the mirror
Seem closer than they appear.
Beneath the lies
Inside the eyes
Of hunger and despair.

Believe half of everything you see
And none of what you hear.
Disfigured image of myself
Staring through a shattered mirror.

Shards of glass began to fall Meant
that I lost a lot over the years.
The broken pieces that were missing
Aren't easily repaired.

Recuperation of the damage done
Will take time to fully heal.

JyJuan Brock

My mistakes gave me hindsight
And the strength to persevere.

Smiles of damaged dreams
Staring through a broken mirror
With clouds forming, Thunder booming.

Lightning flashing in the air
As the water falls
The pain dissolves
Raindrops streaking overhead.

Once the past is washed way
Clouds will slowly disappear
Truth that's told in joking form
Is meant to be concealed.

The hate I feel is everywhere I
can sense it in the air.
If a person shows you who they truly are Beware
of their true intent.

Was given words of wisdom
Knew exactly what they meant
They said.
There's nothing to fear but fear itself.
Be cautious of your peers
Also, facilitate the confidence
While staring through the rear view mirror

The Pen Is The Most Powerful Weapon

If a person senses weakness Or
limitation life adheres.
They'll isolate the weakest link So
stay ten feet ahead.

Forgiveness

Every night before I lay my head down on my pillow
I pray the rain will wash away all the pain and evil spirits,
That's why I get down on my knees and ask God
forgiveness,
Hoping that one day he can release me from the grudges
I've inherit.

Being forgiveness should never be taken as a sign of weakness.
Guilt can paralyze the soul, while becoming detrimental.
Health is more important than any form wealth, which can be
given.

Act like you really want it, and speak it like you really mean
it.
Our sins do not define us; only we define ourselves
Take obligatory steps of caution whist staring deeply down
a well
How can you forgive another soul, if you cannot forgive yourself?

Holding a double standard that is only matched by God himself
Instead I ask you for forgiveness, since I don't want to pronounce
I'm sorry.
Absolution comes from the heart, offering my sincerest apology.

What we are in letters, while we are absent
Is returned in our actions whenever we become present
A heart at peace provides life throughout the body
Forgiveness will open many doors, only if we allow it.

The Pen Is The Most Powerful Weapon

If I can wake with a clean slate, then it must be out of love
Forgive but don't forget, or get your heart involved
The ones that's closest to us, we typically forgive the most
Don't get into the habit of letting emotions show.

We only have one life to live, so living is a must
If I shall die before I wake, I again, ask God for forgiveness.
To have a second chance at life and make things right,
While, not placing yourself in the same position
You can forgive a person and still love them from a distance.

Protecting your position whilst not harboring ill intentions
One thing that I often ask myself that completely forgot to mention.
How can I forgiven, if I can't accept forgiveness?
Love is an emotion, clemency is my intentions
An unexamined life is not a life worth living…

Affirmation: Mathew 6:14-15 For if ye forgive men their trepasses, your heavenly father will also forgive you. But if ye forgive not men their father will also forgive

JyJuan Brock

Poetic Justice

Growing up was taught to never see color,
Only see what's in a person heart
Already at the finish line not knowing where to start
We went from Negros, to Colored, then African Americans
Categorized, according to
The age bracket that we grew up in.

Being branded throughout our oppressions
Seeing as our voices were limited
To minimal forms of self-expression,
Along with the free will of speech
Creatively reciting facts
Intended to make another person think.

What are the universal links, connecting two ethnicities?
Other than the air we breathe and our ability to speak?
Blood coursing through our veins, giving us energy to think
Terrorism became a form of white supremacy.

Black on black crimes became the wars
Fought throughout urban communities
The eyes are the mirror,
Screening everything that we perceive
The freedom of expression can be a powerful weapon Based solely on the audience, and significance of your grievance.

Is it Justice or Just Us?
Perhaps a diverse façade of

The Pen Is The Most Powerful Weapon

Injustice Segregated by the racially biased?
Who wouldn't understand that the change,
In a person's complexion makes one hell of a difference
.How can a man of color go directly to prison?
While carrying the same charges as the opposition.

Instead of being fairly sentenced
While carrying the same charges as the opposition
Instead of being fairly sentenced End up
with lengthy prison sentence
Sending those with the right complexion.

To some different form of therapy or treatment
Alleged that they are the addicts,
But labeling us the drug dealers of the venom
Isolated by complexion

Still living in segregation
Therefore, what really change?
When the equality never add up?
A lot of resentment and hostility
Indisputably begins to build up Attacked
by the same ones
Whose sole duty was to protect us?

Nowaday our children already have the impression
That all cops are bad ones
Shot in the back claiming that it's not because of our color
When a man of different complexion's given sufficient time
to surrender.

JyJuan Brock

All they perceive is black and white, no variation of any other
Trying to shatter my beliefs, but the visions even clearer
When you realize that you are the target
In that reflection in your mirror, Stigmatized
by the public,
Whose focus is only on an image?

But not by the damage, for this irreversible sentence
Constantly stereotyped, never knowing their intentions
Traffic stops that led to gunshots,
Cops are justified for murder
What is justice in that?

When they now become the judge and executioner
That's the difference in how two nationalities had to grow up

We learned to get down on our knees
Pray to God, and ask him for forgiveness
Never taught to hate,
Just survival and a method to escape.

How many chances or risks can we afford to take?
With a human race fueled on anger, criticism, and hate.
In the midst of a world that's designed For
us to fall short anyway.

The Pen Is The Most Powerful Weapon

The Breakdown

When I wasn't living right, my circumstances had to change.
Reality began to show signs of how weak I have became.

No longer using common sense, my thinking was impaired
Focusing too much on the past when the future is straight ahead.
Instead of playing chess, greed over my head
Playing three moves behind, when I should have been ahead.

Gossip will get caught up, with a distortion of the truth Eyes are watching every step, searching for a pattern in how we move.

Coming from an era where loyalties not the same
Best friends will sell you out for a little financial gain
As we grow older, people and priorities tend to change

Damn near brothers growing up, until greed got in the way
Jealousy breeds envy, which helped to ignite a flame.

When its business, never let your feelings get in the way
Greed will keep them loyal as long as you continue to feed them.

The type that couldn't hold weight and never could keep a secret
Once they get all that they can, you'll see a change in their demeanor.

JyJuan Brock

Next to women, money will forever be the route of all evil
Just because they make money together, that doesn't make them your equal.

Grinding without a plan is like having to lose
Show self-confidence, thou you have nothing to prove
If you don't believe in yourself, why should someone else believe in you?

The Pen Is The Most Powerful Weapon

Narcissist

It's tough to deal with people that have a severe sense of entitlement
That spreads like a disease, a wild fire to the environment
Believing the world revolves around them became the basis of their prerogative.

Greatest effort needed to pay inattention to a narcissist
The act of being selfish is just a fraction of their demeanor
Blaming others for certain issues when they were never in attendance.

Patience running thin, from warning signs of repugnance
Their little world is in a bubble bound to burst at any minute. Can't burden nobody but self for making allocated decisions.

Accusatory actions and allegations of their quandary incidents.
Selfish tendencies apparent through the antagonism and resentments.

Acceptance is the key, without harboring agendas.
Word's falling on deaf ear, but it's by choice not to listen
Misery love company, which we learned from the beginning.

Guilt trips starting to limit the conversation we're hearing
Until it's comprehend, that everything is earned and never given

JyJuan Brock

A sense of entitlement, type that will never ask forgiveness
Instead of apologizing they will proceed to pointing fingers
Making rash decisions without any regard to consequences.

Too busy living in the past, when their concern should be focused on the present.
Arrogance growing stronger, showing signs of aggression
Have you ever come across a person who always has a crazy
ass story?

But, while listening even closer, slowly began to understand her motive
While swearing on dead relatives, their kids, mother and fathers.

Making every excuse imaginable as to why they can never come up,
Remaining in indistinguishable situations faulting everyone but self.
Failing to hold accountability. Slowly but surely becoming more than a liability.

Never accepting responsibility for why they're spreading so much misery.
Still not becoming conscious that they are their own worst enemy.

Instead of keeping 100% they'll blame their downfall on society.
This is more than mental health.
Why keep lying to yourself.

The Pen Is The Most Powerful Weapon

What makes these matters worse, is if the one that's a narcissistic. Is the one you perceive every day, and forced to have to deal with?

A casualty of circumstances, knowing that the conceited has predatory issue.
That becomes a detrimental atmosphere to everyone including you!!!

JyJuan Brock

Running the Street

Sometimes in life, there will be a road that you'll have to walk alone.
To learn from life experiences, while coming into our own.
The die has been cast numbers are still unknown Crawling before we walked, each day became a stepping stone.

Often pulling all-nighters, even in the bitter cold
Rain, sleet, snow, or hail, on the corner is where we stood
Nosey neighbors calling the law, assuming that we were marketing drugs.

Started off as kids, until curiosity got the best of us Becoming acclimated to our surrounding, while slowly claiming our innocence.
Growing up fast, females, and money became a way to motivate us.

Orajel and dry bread, knotted baggies trying to come up
Watchful eyes over the old heads, waiting for our opportunity to blow up.

With open ears and closed mouth, try paying closer attention. The game is never complimentary but it's priceless if you own it
By learning the formula, you'll stay one stride ahead of your opponents.

The Pen Is The Most Powerful Weapon

Mature enough to be harassed, but too young for an indictment.
Reckless progress of excitement, turn to resentment and violence
Law enforcement intimidate us for loitering, taking the trust away.

Major concern was to strip us from society, by tossing us inside a cage.
Stereo-typed at such a young age, became detrimental towards the pain.

Stating that the lack of parental guidance,
Turned us into products of our environment
Not considering that police harassing our youth didn't play a big part in it.

Being publically profiled, rebelling against authority
That doesn't make any sense; it that's no ethnic profiling then let us know what it is?
Instead of utilizing public resources, like in suburban communities.

They'll sit and hang us out to dry like a set of dirty sheets
Only attention was to lock us up and throw the key away
We started idolizing the streets, hoping one day to be free.

For those without a father, the streets became their dad
Studying neighborhood hustlers, trying to master their craft
Always told if you don't finish first, you'll always finish last.

JyJuan Brock

Once you're knee deep in the game, and get your first package in your hand.
Starting with just a gram, but praying on a hundred grand
The trap game takes your virtuousness, forcing you to become a man.

With a loaded gun on your waist, and a pocket full of cash
Becomes a recipe for disaster, feeling the clout that you never had.

A hustler that never sleeps, all about supply and demand
Ducking and dodging the police, hop out boys on our ass
Sneaky friends and stick up boy trying to come up off your stash.

In this game don't trust a soul, watch out for snakes in the grass Close friends become envious, clocking another person's cash.
Jail or death is imminent when playing Russian roulette

Running in place, no progress made, and still finishing last
Thinking it's a rat race, hustle at your own pace Moving too fast could result in making detrimental mistakes.

All because you didn't want to place second in another man's face.
How this system is set up cops make millions of mistakes
But, we can't afford one slip up that will put our lives at stake. No half stepping

When time is of the essence!!!

The Pen Is The Most Powerful Weapon

Raw Emotions

Raw emotions help ignite the flame
With embers burning from desire
In the end there's no one else to blame.
Once fuel is added to the fire,
That's why it's best to make a change
There's only two ways out the game.

Either death or penitentiaries
Mind swerving in and out of lanes
Don't become a distant memory
Behind prison walls with bullet scars
That shows exactly who you are
Curtains depicted is prison bars.

Precious moment lost
Both near and far
How much strength does it really take?
To catch yourself a falling star.

With complacency and lucid dreams
Dreadful memories
From all the things we've seen
Don't try to live a double life Stay focused on reality.

Or end up in a sinking boat
Drifting down a lonely stream

JyJuan Brock

Prepared me to be a man

Life lessons that are being taught
Was more than just for me?
Longevity and Legacy's
Are more important than they seem

It's like a roller coaster ride
Or climbing up your family tree
It takes a town to raise a child I
wished the same applied to me.

I became the rotten apple
That fell the furthest from the tree
Decaying scars beneath the flesh
Made it hard for eyes to see.

A hollowed shell outside the walls of hell
Hoping one day to be free
The worms inside ate me alive
And stole my whole identity
Choices I've made were mine alone So
there's no one to blame but me.

Transparent like an open book
For the entire world to see I pray
events that I've been through
Will make myself a better me

I let them take my dignity
They couldn't take my pride

The Pen Is The Most Powerful Weapon

Pain helps a person to adapt
Experience will teach you to survive
What good is learning from mistakes?
If you're still living a lie.

Unresolved Issue

Our limitation only live inside of our mind
Time is very costly; don't waste it living someone else's
life Everything we've ever wanted is on the differing
side of fear.
Once courage is achieved, you can conquer even your worst
nightmares.
Cannot place another person in a category, they can't even place
themselves.
Harboring ill feeling is damaging to your health
Hatred and envy rots the bones, at times it's hard to
conceal.

In time, all open wounds will gradually begin to heal
Unrealistic expectation on people who lack integrity and morals.
Becomes a recipe for disaster, hurting you to the core But
if you distinguish how these people act, self- inflicting
older scars.

Admitting to self, because you knew exactly who they were
A person can only achieve or vocalize what you consent for
them to do.
Options are always open, only you can prevent the negativity
that ensures.
Giving up to much energy to the ones who have the least to lose.

For a lack of better words, if you're in pain, they won't lose any
sleep.

The Pen Is The Most Powerful Weapon

Life is all on what we make it, always has, always will be
Sometimes the warning sign are there, but it's by choice for you to see.

The best revenge is mass success, but that comes from patients and forgiveness
Life is 10% of what happens, an 90% of how we react to it
If you take gaze on what you attained in life,

You'll always have more than you could ever want
Yet, if you capture a glance of what you don't have,
You will never have enough.

Misplaced Anger

An individual cannot change anything in life you don't to acknowledge.
Walk a mile in another's shoes before you criticize their problems.
Whatever is begun with anger, will end in shame shortly after.
Time to change the page at its ending and begin with a new chapter.
Anger may possibly ruin interactions leaving you as the sole person to suffer.

Start form where you are. Use what you have, but still pray for proper guidance.
Misplaced anger speed racing, navigating with no direction
However, the mind is sober enough not to make any major infractions.
Remember, that with every action, there will always be a reaction.

Keep your eyes and ears focused, on where they both belong.
On your own decisions and behaviors being faced here and now.
Resentment will have your thoughts irrational, believing you shouldn't throw in the towel.
At the very core, it's human nature to blame other human beings.
It becomes an essential self -preservation tactic to try to escape accountability.

Don't want to unleash your issues out on another just for a means for a release.
Positivity brings energy, which leaves your mind at ease

The Pen Is The Most Powerful Weapon

Do not allow yourself to be the rabid dog fighting to break the leash.
When a dog bites another person, he or she is immediately put to sleep.

JyJuan Brock

Coming to Terms

In existence we pray for the best, while expecting the worse
Read between the lines because there's truth behind every word.
We all have dreams that money can't but, those are the ones we want.

Money can't buy happiness, with that I came to terms
Happiness isn't ready made, it comes from within ourselves
If you're aiming for the moon, you will see stars along the way.
Strive not to be a successful, but be a man of value, and of desirable qualities.

Don't make excuses, find alternative solutions.
The hardest part of learning something new, is unlearning the old way of doing it.
Life is about making an impact, not based on another's financial gratuity.
All the money in the world, doesn't characterize a person's personality.

Possessions never make a man and money isn't everything
Can't take it with you when you're in jail, dying, or deceased.
The value of life is measured by means of priceless memories,
Creating lifelong recollections, intended to exist for all eternity.

While maturing as a whole and building strong ties and relationships.
It proves that we are not a product of or situations But creation of our decisions.

The Pen Is The Most Powerful Weapon

Coming to terms with who you are, there is no pun intended.

Everything has a breaking point, and every person has their limits. Whether irrational or not, the ball is always in our court

Learning to trust instinct is a perfect way to start. Existence is perceived differently, depending on the eye of the beholder.

People often say that motivation doesn't last forever However, with an appetite for massive success, A person must keep their hunger.

JyJuan Brock

L.O.E.
LOYALTY OVER EVERYTHING

Building a solid bond that strengthens the weaker links.
Because a person isn't blood, doesn't make them less family
Understand the underlying meaning of what that word really means.

More than just declaration, it's a lifestyle most use the implication sparingly.
Money is monetary, but loyalty is everything
Growing up you were taught that you cannot choose who's your family.

Whomever made that initial assessment, created a powerful analogy.
There is not a lineage franchise where you are drafted to a team.

Nor can you do any trading to alter your family tree
The only exception to that rule is creating your own dynasty.

Loyalty, trust, and love should come above everything Always the ones you least suspect, to go above and beyond for those beliefs.

More than just a way of life when building a legacy
Instilling proper morals is more than just a common courtesy.
Screaming until you're blue in the face
Loyalty Over Everything!!!

The Pen Is The Most Powerful Weapon

The Man in the Mirror

Introduced to a new acquaintance a friend of mine insisted I'd meet.
Asking if we were of any relation because the two of us could pass for family.

Same first name as if he'd stolen my identity
Inquiring as to what area he grew up in; his response was right inside of me.

Skeptical of his attentions, so I listened quietly.
Trying to spot any in discrepancies assuming that there has to be.
His mannerism and character held distinctive similarities
Our dispositions were the same along with his mental creativity.

Knowing my darkest secrets, I never even told my family
As if we knew each other our entire life with an ambiance of familiarity.
Appearance vaguely familiar though age considerably.

The mirror image staring back was a replication of me shocked momentarily and unable to speak.
Getting light headed, confused, and a little weak in the knees.

He was divulging my mind and my eyes to an unusual side of reality.

JyJuan Brock

Depicting the turmoil my life was headed but I was too naive to see.
Not allowing my heart, to become engulfed; with negativity and greed.

See my hands, reach out your hand and put it into my side, stop doubting and believe.
The man that I was speaking to was a reflection of me.

The Pen Is The Most Powerful Weapon

Federal Nightmare

Federal examination are serious accusations
Indictments are under seal until reaching initial arraignment stages
Detention hearing will determine existing factors and condition

To establish if you're going home, or being remanded to the Bureau of Prison.
Filing rule 16 to uncap the major factors of your criminal charges.

All accusations held until the burden proof is determined
Once the discoveries produced go over every solitary page with your lawyer.

Confer with every option; has the DA has presented any plea bargain?
Using caution while talking, lips may be closed but cars are always open.

The memorandum has every count sited against you on the indictment.
Prevaricate on whether to take the plea, or roll the dice and attempt to fight them.
Be precise and understand that it's your life that's up for auction.

Your relevant conduct establishes your limited choice in options.

Wanting to make an example out of anyone apposing their power
Don't become a target for as judicator, D.A. or U.S. Marshalls.
Their point system is complicated, leaving the smartest of lawyers baffled.

Laws are changing all the time, and can be difficult to keep up with
Feds can use any prior charges, carrying a prison term of at least a year and a day.
From old state or county convictions, that debts have already been paid.

841 and 51's doubling the sentencing guidelines on a case
Category and offense level can jump from 51 up to 38
Changing your sentence from a few months into couple of decades.

The federal courts have the funding and resources that we cannot contain.
For every crime committed resulting in a conviction Used to calculate your offense level along with any other enhancements.

Departures rarely given only under extreme circumstances
95% conviction rate, because most are afraid to fight

The Pen Is The Most Powerful Weapon

How can you fault someone when the high end or their sentence is life?

JyJuan Brock

80's Babies

Born in the 80's but grew up in the 90's
Generational gap became the last of a dying breed Almost everyone had a pager; cell phone were nearly nonexistent.

It wasn't that we couldn't get them, they were just too expensive
Payphones were everywhere, a quarter for 15 minutes
Local hustlers would utilize those to conduct illegal business.

Around this time was the height of crack epidemic
Mother forced to play both positions,
Since fathers lacked in attendance

Too many were too inconsistent.
Most were either getting high, in a grave, or in prison
Prisoners of our circumstances, yet still stigmatized by the system.

This was the world 80's babies were forced to live in
My first addiction, B.B. guns, and ice cream
After that it was light skinned girls and parties
Crack began wreaking havoc on our low income communities.
While the upper class society were gifted geographical immunity.

Recognize the brutality of the urban economy

The Pen Is The Most Powerful Weapon

Distressing only generations at the lower end of poverty
The term "80's Babies", refers to adolescences wedged within a vicious cycle.

Watching men and women sell their souls for pennies on the dollar.
Several kids started selling the same poison that their parents were chasing after.

A life raft to keep from drowning in the drug polluted waters.
Admiration turned from drowning in the drug polluted waters.

Admiration turned into hatred from the ones we used to look up to.
How can you respect a person that lost all of their dignity and morals?
Having to practice what they preached and learn to lead by example.

Instead the monkey's weighing heavy their shoulder, still chasing behind the devil.
Slowly peeling away the layers, while focusing on the bigger picture.
Millions affected by this crisis, which spread throughout the nation.

Experimental guinea pigs due to government because of political connections.
With total disregard of everyone that's been affected.

JyJuan Brock

Dirty needles and crack pipes littered all over the projects
In schoolyards and playgrounds, every place you can imagined.

Our choices in role models became slim and indifferent
Limited to actors, rappers, athletes or local street pharmacists.
Slowly causing genocide throughout our neighborhoods at the cost of our expense.

Brain washed to believe that were the cause of this catastrophic pandemic.
Disregarding men, woman, and snatching the virtue of our children.
If you ask me they knew what they were doing from the beginning.

The devastation left behind we won't soon forget it
Traumatized the innocent, all for their benefit. These are the nature of concerns this era is still dealing with.

Welcome to the 80's

The Pen Is The Most Powerful Weapon

Was it Really Worth It?

As a child, no one ever imagined prison as being a part of their future.
Never considered throughout your past, now you have a different outlook.
In the eyes of the youth, prison was a place for bad people who did awful things.
However, some aren't as terrible as the public makes them out to be.

Most do it for survival, to find an end to their means
Never judging a book, nothing is ever as it seem.
Becoming your worst nightmare, or most pleasing fantasy
How did you end up at this point? Was it couiosity, or out of greed?

Maybe all of the above with everything in-between
Learning the hard way how to deal with humiliation and humility.
In the left hand there was no love, on the other, is pure stupidity.
Brain functions are on "E" with no breathing space for creativity.

Long ways from perfect, though, twice as close to home
The steel doors of prison eat away at the mind, body, and soul.

JyJuan Brock

How could your mind ever deceive you in such a way?
When things we once considered sturdy and dependable swept away.

At what point does a man stop analyze the situation?
Reality sets in at the mere thought of the time you could be facing stripped away from family, was the reward truly worth the risk?

Doing the bid would be easier if the circumstances were different.
Instead, your actions forced you to live in in-deplorable conditions.

Where a light bit can easily turn into an irrevocable sentence.
Sound advice is only good if you take heed to the words of wisdom.

The Pen Is The Most Powerful Weapon

Choose your Path

Angels, were created with purpose and reason but no desire Creative thinking inspires ideas, giving courage to fly higher.

Destination towards the clouds, then the stars shortly after Choices that we make us who we are, choose wisely before you answer.

Animals were created with desire but no reason.
Survival by any means without compassion for the living.
Man on the other hand, carries both genetic qualities
Rationalized thinking and multiple personalities.

Half of the solution to any problem lies to defining it.
You can't really make progress against a problem, until you understand what it is.

Therefore, if a man's reason is stronger than his desire, he will analyze and circumvent.
However, if his desire is stronger than his reason, it's due in part to lack of common since.
It is not the load that break you down, it is more so how you carry it.

Prosperity has always risen from the ground up, unearthing a timeline that's been inherited.
Education is critical, attempting to accomplish more than our successors.
Aspiration for success should be greater than your initial fear of failure.

JyJuan Brock

Attribute: your success to this, never give or take any excuses.
The most important thing is that you try, dream big or dare to be unsuccessful.

We can choose a path of war and unilateral actions
Outlook danger in the eyes with hope and pure satisfaction
Choose your path!!!

The Pen Is The Most Powerful Weapon

Sibling Rivalry

We can easily forgive a child who is afraid of the dark;
What's the difference when two siblings begin to grow apart?
Shedding light on the situation, still not knowing where to start.

The real misfortune is when you're so afraid of the light;
You'll keep yourself in the dark.
Lights getting dimmer, nights getting a little colder
Adapting to life while hauling the entire world on your shoulders.

Prior to us knowing what a friend was, we were each other's best friend.
With a five year age difference.
Nevertheless, that didn't make me look at him any different.

Our mother taught us to always be each other's keeper
That was a promise she made us say, and was my full intention to keep it.
We used to ride or die together and maintain each other's secrets.

Even though she told me not to, I still treated him as my equal
Started getting a little older becoming teenager
I could no longer tell him all my secrets.

JyJuan Brock

That's when situations began to change and circumstances got deeper.

Our interests were the initial fixation that became different
He was still into sports; my vice was the streets and teenage women.
He didn't understand; I although we were blood siblings,
My lust for women changed the game.

As I came into my own, all he wanted to do was follow me
I'm sure we all been there before.
Unless you were the youngest in the family
Then you wouldn't understand the typical case of sibling rivalry.

Fact is, what I just stated became the recipe for animosity
The most complex thing is the decision to act, the rest is sheer persistence.
Treated him as me equal for so long that he didn't know the different.

All I could do is blame myself, for being placed in this position.
Sometimes I wish my stubborn ass had listened
Instead I have to face the monster that I myself created

Affirmation: 1Corinthian 13:4 Love is patient and kind, Love does not envy or boast, its not arrogant or rude; It does not rejoice at wrong doing, but rejoice the truth.

The Pen Is The Most Powerful Weapon

Addicted

We started off as close friends
Type of connection that should have never happened
Used to date each other over the years mostly socially
You were my party girl, and the life of every party
Who knew the day would come when we'd become frienemies

Distant memories, of how much you really meant to me
Not healthy for each other, exhausting all of my energy
Ruined relationships with both my friends and with my family .

At the time, you were a shoulder of relief when I was down and out
Friends never understood as to why I kept you around,
Telling me every day that everything will be alright
Knew she was lying by the way she tucked me in at night
Engaging scent of your perfume seeping out of my pores
You wanted nothing more than to allow yourself an open door

Partying all night while still making love to each other
Pillow talking while under the covers
Getting jealous when your advancements were geared towards my brother

JyJuan Brock

My life in turmoil I had to get my shit together
My mother disapproved, knowing that I could do better
Addicted to her that's why I wrote myself this love letter
Because I'm Addicted

The Pen Is The Most Powerful Weapon

Part of the Game

In the streets, relationship is tempting but often scary
Emotions fully exposed to the elements, unable to use rationale thinking.

Female love is rare and between often become temporary
Life is excellent as long as everyone is winning
When circumstances change, you'll see those people change dramatically.

When they are no longer receiving a salary
Everyone wants to be on the winning until that team start losing.
The thought of jail sends everyone into frenzy and a state of full confusion.

Knowing the consequences of the game, no one forcing them into it.
What was once your Queen became as distant as your homies?

Claiming to be something she's not, the proof was in the pudding.

Not having to say a word their actions already proved it
Shortly after, those same individuals start searching for a means to escape.

JyJuan Brock

Rushing water has the potential too very whelm that's standing in its way.

Bringing up situations from years ago, with accusatory claims.

Alleging that prior instances were excuse enough to justify their ways.
As if their heart begun to freeze, gradually extinguishing the flame.

In spite of the situation, things will never be the same
Every man makes mistakes, but only fools make the same mistake twice.
Don't gamble with a woman when you already gambled with your life.

Prepare yourself for paycheck; it's probably gonna tear you apart.
Just pray that you're strong enough to take the pain that you dished out.
They will stalk and wait until you're at your lowest point ever
Then they'll drop a bomb on you. you'll lucky if you even get a letter.

Or an explanation, as to if the love was real or if she found another hustler.
That fulfills all of her financial greed and is dumb enough to let her.

The Pen Is The Most Powerful Weapon

While telling yourself;
If you knew better you would have done better!

In its place, notes full or hatred instead of a love letter
Regretting the day you thought you found the one and fell in love with her.

Was always told, the same way you got her will be the same way you'll lose them.
Mad at yourself for being blind to what your friends were telling you.
Pride and emotion to precedence, that's something a man, should never do.
But guess what?
That's all a part of the game!

JyJuan Brock

Correction

The eraser in its truest form, was created by total accident.
Bread crust, were initially used, to remove inscriptions
from different documents.
Picking up a piece of latex rubber by mistakes,
Before noticing the slip-up it was already too late.

It left behind rubber crumbs, which was easily swept away
A little bit of history from Britain 1770,
To help corrective errors while using as an apology.
With people too, even the worst errors of our lives, can be corrected if we try.

If you crave something bad enough, it's worth putting up a fight.
Re-familiarize yourself with the struggle No
heat, no lights, and cold water.
Remembering how it felt, should be inspiration to progress even further.

When life gives you lemons, don't allow anything in your way.
Instead, turn those same lemons into a glass of lemonade

So forget the stress, you should want to see yourself at your best.
The value of a person's friendship, and true character, put to the ultimate test.
If they leave you at your worst, there is no need to want them back.

The Pen Is The Most Powerful Weapon

Put away all of the childish ways while never turning back
Bury it deep within, making sure to lay those thoughts to rest.
Kill them with kindness while sending them to a better place.

Government

The world that we live in Men,
women, and children.
Where people are judged
By the places they live in.

The rich will get richer
That's the design of our system.
Categorized by our race
Our beliefs and religion.

Just because we're alive
Doesn't mean that we're living.
Stereotyped by the law
While not given a reason.

Targeting blacks and claiming we look suspicious
If that's not racism, then tell me what is it?
Modern Day Slavery, nothing much has been changed
They still leave us in bondage while
Shackled and chained
They'll keep building more jail
That detained 90% minorities, and 10% white men
I'm far from racist, just speaking truth from my wisdom
On how the laws is one sided
That's realities image
The life that is led
From a corrupted system

The Pen Is The Most Powerful Weapon

H.A.L.T

Hungry. Angry. Lonely. Tired.
The stomach begins to touch, reaching well beyond the vertebrae.
Fall seven times and stand up eight, due to part to lack of energy.

A trickling, effect, both mentally and physically
Cerebral agitation because of others selfish tendencies
Spiritually exhausted from weighty options and responsibilities.
Get rid of insecurities while locating life's inconsistencies

In the end, there will be no type of spiritual connection.
Devious tongues manipulated by means of conversation.
Exhausting when individuals assume they can easily take advantage.
While trying to comprehend the intentions behind their actions.

Equally, we may look at the same image, that doesn't imply we both will like it.
The same holds true with watch and every moment that life gives us.
If you don't step up and fight for you, no one will do it for you.
Well done is better than well said, within yourself you must be truthful.

JyJuan Brock

Get real about your life and everyone that is place in it.
Be truthful about what working in your life; stop making excuses on what isn't.

Recognize that your perceptions may be vastly different,
Open your eyes to what causes all of your anger and resentment.

Capture the power back from those whom have hurt you. All emotions of the human catalog, hate, anger, and resentment are amongst the most destructive Awakened by those you distinguish to have hurt you or those whom you are truly in love with.

Without occasional pain, we wouldn't recognize and appreciate pleasure.
Whatever begun in anger will end in shame and will live with you forever.

The Pen Is The Most Powerful Weapon

Shelter From The Storm

We might think that words of encouragement is merely saying something courteous.
If we think that way, we fall short to recognize the lasting power it possesses.

Trembling at the thought of being in the mist of stormy weather.
A raincoat, some rain boots, and maybe an umbrella, Life's tempest can come in many forms; so much we value swept away in a distant.

The downpour takes us out of our comfort zone to show us new beginnings,
Rationalized that presence of difficulty is more of s curse than a blessing.
Now is the time to keep focus, don't agonize yourself over material possessions.

To stretch us, and to help us grow, doesn't mean the absence of hope.
Suspended in the air, the murky clouds are still afloat.

Tempting to believe that our trouble directs our story of our lives.
The dark vapors above our heads as if the sky is about to cry.

As the starts falling in the clouds, representing the past,

JyJuan Brock

Present and future tears that have jet to shed

Hard to recognize how much pain was weighing down on our hands.

When one hurts, we all hurts, we're now in this by ourselves.
Protectors and providers to the ones we love the most,
You got my back and I got yours.
 I could be the shelter and shields you from the storm
Situations only continue if we allow it to ensure.

There is nothing left to prove but also everything to lose
Encourage those that has been impacted by ghastly conditions.
Sometimes life seems far too short and full of complications.

We can trust that all lives have purpose and significance
Do you hear me? Are you listening, that is a momentous difference?

Be lead by dreams in your heart, neither of us can define.
Understanding the first step, and only with acceptance can there be recovery.
Sometimes that storm that came along meant to wash away the pain that's inside of us.

Truly sympathetic how life can drain the passions from our lives.
A single teardrop slowly falls from the corner of her eye.
Recuperations take a while but all we have is time,

The Pen Is The Most Powerful Weapon

With acceptance and the will to persevere without shelter to run inside.
At the end of every storm, the sun makes his presence shine.

JyJuan Brock

Perseverance

It all started as a discussion one that I won't soon forget
Guaranteeing me to find the "one" that outshines all of the rest.
Forgetting our petty differences without wondering what was next.
Giving the proper guidance, while telling me I'm the best.

You used to hold me you taught me to live with my regrets
To the beholder, the eye recognizes a person's strength
Appreciate a person by not undermining their confidence

Everyone love a shining star, especially if they're winning the race.
When that state no longer shines, the truth will shine through in its place.
It's all about finding the right balance even in the midst of hate.
The sweetness of a good heart a wolf can smell from miles away.

Channel positive energy, take a challenges that are worthwhile and beneficial.
People will walk over you like a doormat only if you allow them.
Your heart isn't for everyone; must be earned from the beginning.

The Pen Is The Most Powerful Weapon

The same goes for respect, you have to give it to receive it
Become comfortable even in the most uncomfortable situations.
Why have sex with their body with no physical attachment? When you can make love to the mind for decades of satisfaction.

Dark

"Repent" means to reverse direction
The same discretion applied for self-preservation Years of ongoing suffering and total isolation.

Pain masked by piercings, bearings, tattoos, and gauges.
Darkness consumes the sky, typically in different stages
So many existent wounds caused by words of mental desertion.
Death doesn't enclose the last remark, but it does with resurrection.

The potential risk of our language can cause a person everlasting damage.
Who's pulling the thread of string if the puppet master is absent?
While calling the tongue, a relentless evil full of deadly poison and brutal lashing.

Experiencing pain that seems endless, with situations that appear hopeless.
When the odds are stacked against, we begin to lose focus.

Feeling trapped while overdosing on a series of emotions
Even when catastrophes are a direct result of our own rebellion.

We still should have an escape plan just in case things get hectic.

The Pen Is The Most Powerful Weapon

Find the same joy and freedom parting with a false sense of protection.

Instead of running to places that entrap us or being ruled by our fears and addictions.

JyJuan Brock
The Pen Is The Most Powerful Weapon

Denial

In the real world, the rear view mirror is always clearer than the windshield.
Debris and grime accumulating may be too much for some to handle.
Learning how to mount, and learning how to dismantle

Contradiction separates the soul, with accusatory actions
Throughout every transformation there has always been one constant:
That's the advancement of opportunity which has a slim degree of options.
No one's existence is too bad to fix, and it is never too late to fix it.

Denial is what kills dreams, hopes, and different aspirations.
Or might have been real chance to overcome a serious disaster.

Cannot afford the luxury of defensiveness nor the deception of denial.
Seeing people succumb to these sad effects because they failed to recognize the problem.
Sweeping it under the rug, becoming blind to the signals that are right in our face.

Excuses amount to nothing, and leads to bridges to nowhere.

The Pen Is The Most Powerful Weapon

Those whom specialize in using them, will never develop awareness
What people want is not the truth, but social validation.

To justify their denying way while addressing the public, These problems do not get better in time, you can't change what's not acknowledged, and what we don't acknowledge, will only get worse until we do something about it.

Take off those rose colored glasses, and see the world for exactly what it's worth.
Those unwilling to consciously identify their negative behaviors with, the negative characteristics within their life's pattern.

Will never rationalize what denial is doing to their life's progressive values

JyJuan Brock

Another look/racial profiling

Take another look into the depths of our society.
Senseless shooting by the police, but is there any validity?
Ones that took that oath to protect and serve slowly
became the public enemy.

Hiding behind a badge, protective immunity
Living above the law, obstructing justice in our
communities.
Upon proper inspection, tell me exactly what you see?
Citizens on patrol abusing their authority.
Yet another obstacles due to unforgiving police brutality
Blue code of silence and stop snitching are one in the same
analogy.

Only difference, the who are categorized to justify their
means.
To the law, we are hindering apprehensive for not telling
them anything.
Nevertheless, they're doing the same thing, only for a
different team.

Where is the justification? Where they can do it but we
can't?
Ethnic profiling and all pain that the ghetto brings. Is
barely enough to say that we're living the American
Dream.
More like living in a nightmare, parked on the corner of
Elm Street.

The Pen Is The Most Powerful Weapon

The public cannot afford to make a solitary mistake
All it takes is one incident for the courts to lock us away
The police on the other hand, can afford to make millions of mistakes.
With little to no consequence or repercussion foe any actions they may take.

Black guy in a white neighborhood, sticks out like a sore thumb
Pulled over for a (DWB) assuming they have either drugs or guns.

White guy in a black community, also sticks out like a sore toe
Pulled over for (DWW) assuming they're coming to buy drugs.

Two different scenarios but actually both the same
Both stereotyped and classified based on the complexion of our skin.

JyJuan Brock

Untitled

Contentment isn't a remark that I frequent from day to day
Apart from when it's pertaining to family and unconditional love that I contain.

Compliancy becomes a prison injected directly into the human brain.
No since in arguing, there mind is already made.

One that's content with who they are, refusing to ever change.
Those are the unchanged public that still stuck in their ways Most will only change if it's for monetary gain.

Though we may breathe the same air, we will never be the same.
Maliciousness is an inherent trait, try to stay far away.
Having realistic expectations, knowing exactly what can change.

While also realizing that no two people are the same
Instigate your intellect into a diverse mind-frame
Once a person shows his or her true color, grab the canvas and can of paint.

Embark on painting the image those folks tried to portray
Freely expressing through abstract art, the hate, and the envy show on the canvas.

The Pen Is The Most Powerful Weapon

Harboring ill thoughts now becomes irrelevant
Those individuals showed you who they were; yet, still didn't want to believe it.

Still try to remain your close friend, as long as they comprise something to profit.

JyJuan Brock

Prepare Me to Be a Man

Life lessons that are being taught
Was more than just for me?
Longevity and Legacies
Are more important than they seem.

It's like a roller coaster ride
Or climbing up your family tree
It takes a town to raise a child
I wished the same applied to me.

I became the rotten apple
That fell the furthest from the tree
Decaying scars beneath the flesh
Made it hard for eyes to see.

A hollowed shell outside the walls of hell
Hoping one day to be free
The worms inside ate me alive
And stole my who identity.

Choices I've made were mine alone
So there's none to blame but me
Transparent like an open book For
the entire world to see.

I pray events that I've been through
Will make myself a better me
Processing thoughts within my brain
Comprehending what they really mean.

The Pen Is The Most Powerful Weapon

From time to time I ask myself
Why can't this all be a dream?
The best questions are the ones that doesn't need to be explained.

Mothers only want what's best
For the children that she's birthed,
I've made myself a statistic
And the situation worse.

One thing that she's always said
Proved the truth can really hurt,
Was that she's rather see me in a cell
Than six feet in the dirt.

No mother wants their child to die
Behind the lifestyle that they've chose
You have to play the hand that's dealt And
pray you never lose.

Rose pedals for every tear that fell,
While giving sound advice
All the years of fallen tears, Along
with sleepless nights.

But when understood her logic And
could fully comprehend. Some things
she's said when I was young So today
I'm becoming a man.

JyJuan Brock

Can I Explain Myself

The life questions are the ones that doesn't need to be explained.
Life's most precious moments intended to take our breath away.

Greed on the other hand is even harder to escape
Lack of confidence in themselves, that never gives but quick to take.

Examine between the lines; gaze through a few chapters
Does the reward outweigh the risk? Have you calculated the factors?

Playing Rush Roulette, the odds designed to be stacked against us.
Five rounds in the revolver, one solitary bullet absent.

Chamber loaded one by one, bullets slowly spinning in rotation.
What are the probabilities of landing on the only empty chamber?
One thing about money, it has no remorse and carries no discretion.

No loyalty to any one yet everyone can possess it
Doesn't matter a person's creed. ethnicity, or religion.
If anything, currency produced greed into existence.

The Pen Is The Most Powerful Weapon

Money isn't everything; let not soul tell you different.
What is existence without its risk? Are you aware of what you're risking?

Yesterday's news isn't selling today's papers.
You were who you were, even before you ever got there
You can change your outer shell, but that's only the top layer.

Intelligence is a terrible thing to waste, yet the most influential weapon.
Will power is an emotional fuel that can run out at any second.
The only way to guarantee forward growth during these downward progressions.
Is to devise a strategic plan that sustains the energy to thrust us in the right direction.

The number one fear amongst all people is rejection.
The number two need among people is to feel accepted
What is our sole purpose?
Do you see the credits rolling?

Looking at a glass that's half-full, while others see it as half empty.
Directing a motion picture that's depicting your life story.
Already seen the beginning up to the middle of the movie judging by a person's actions, it's not hard to predict the ending.
It's is at the very core of human nature to deflect responsibility.

JyJuan Brock

Fundamental self-preservation trying to escape accountability.
Pipes bursting under pressure, losing sight of their identity.
When those silver metal bracelets clasped tightly around the wrist,
You'll exactly the type of people that you've been dealing with.
Life flashes before their eyes, which comes to no surprise hiding behind a disguise never fully understand why.

The Pen Is The Most Powerful Weapon

True Love Has No Limitations

The seeds been planted, two lovers can thrive in peace
Plenty of rain and sunshine enables them to flourish properly.
On top of the highest mountain, for the entire world to see,
A flower that blooms unwavering in the eyes of adversity
Blossoms of so beautiful, becoming an even rarer commodity.

Completely sought after, its essence has the most desirable qualities.
Almost as if it were a legend, no one ever gets to see.
Possibilities are endless, no limitations overseen.

Enjoy life in all its glory, a little love, a little laughter.
Praying that this love story ends with happily ever after.
Never thinking that I would find someone so beautiful and kind.

Destiny insures that one day and you'll finally be mine.
When two unite as one and both lives intertwine,
Finding the match to park the flame of love within our lives.

Whispering sweet nothings, because you are truly one of a kind.
Compassion throbbing throughout our hearts, the glimmers sparkle in her eyes.

JyJuan Brock

As if we wished upon a shooting star to fall directly from the sky.

Hold on to that star with all your might, true love is hard to find.

If I fell she became my crutch that kept me off the ground
The completion of a broken heart since all of the pieces has been found.

Our conversations are like foreplay on the mind, when we're together our loves deeper.
If I had then she had, If she had it was vice versa.
Understanding each other's problems and accepting one another.

That type of love is all anyone could ever ask for. You won't know what true love is until it comes knocking at the door.

Pounding do severe it's almost impossible to ignore
Adrenaline flowing through your bone, a sensation no one could mistake.
An itch that needed scratched, and I chill we couldn't shake.

Now when I call your name, your face suddenly appears
We can feel the love surrounding us, relinquishing all our fears.

Looking back over the years, although our scars have healed

The Pen Is The Most Powerful Weapon

It is our time for utter happiness, we earned for each and every tear.

I tell myself time and time again, this time is our time to win.
Because our hearts are genuine and our love is heaven sent

Moreover, in the course of a thorough investigation
We both began to realize that, True love has no limitations.

JyJuan Brock

Don't Judge Me By My Mistakes, Judge Me By My Character

Judging a person solely on their past, doesn't delineate their true character.
Stereotypical way of thinking, no person was ever born on a pedestal.

Instead of evaluating a book exclusively by its cover, maybe read the entire story.
Of the hardships, the struggles, even some of their successes.
Get to be acquainted with the person and not just by their circumstances.

An individual cannot see who we are, if they focus too much on who we were.
If asked to present society. The response would beg to differ.
Open your eyes and distinguish that there are two sides to every playing field.
You may play for a winning team, but even the best can be defeated on a whim.

Being branded and categorized as if we are uncivilized.
Acknowledge only by our mistakes, never the constructive side.
How is a person supposed to prosper if incapable to thrive and live a normal life?
So instead of being honest, became dishonest, their entire livelihood became a lie.

The Pen Is The Most Powerful Weapon

Giving society what they want while hiding behind a façade.
Discouraging positive progress and deterring people from being who they truly are.
Life built from mistakes that make human errors differentiate.

A word of encouragement from a complete stranger could give you the courage to succeed.
Moral support from a spouse can give you a better understanding to his or her personals needs.

Love from a parent can inspire you to reach your full potential.
Understanding from society would prove that we're all created equal.
Wouldn't you want a second chance if placed in the same position?

Options are limited because of our past predicaments
Making it harder and harder by the day.
Criminal background hindering the chances of getting a decent wage,
The American standard of stigmatizing and segregation takes that all away.
They want to keep us criminals without an outlet to escape.

JyJuan Brock

Prisoner In My Mind

If you cannot think outside the box, all you'll ever see is four corner.
When the mind is running wild, it's hard to maintain focus on what's really important.
One man's prison became another man's armor
A monetary lapse can impair a person's judgement.

From outside looking in, the box is a form of disciplinary correction.
But from the inside looking out, it shows a diversified perception.
No one is immune to the lies and lures of temptation.
Maneuver through situations where the mind's easily persuaded.

Allowing a fool to make a mockery by conveying the message.
Might as well cut yours ties and connections for entertaining that method.
No person is your acquaintance, who demands your utter silence,
Succumbing to ignorance breeds a history of violence.

Fire of the heart sends smoke directly to the head.
A livid person will devise the best speech they'll forever regret.
Learning the influence of love and the limitations of belligerence.

The Pen Is The Most Powerful Weapon

You can always learn from circumstance, despite the consequence.
When passion meets motivation and fixation is born,
No matter how high you get in life, never forget where you came from.
From that tiny crack in the box, the radiance of freedom shined right in.
Giving a glimmer of hope toward humility rather than one of prominence.

Arguing with the ignorant, creates more ignorance than common sense.
Becoming a prisoner of the mind by underestimating the opponent.
No honor amongst thieves, though the eyes don't always show it.
They are the mirror of the soul that serves their sole purpose.

JyJuan Brock

Understanding Priorities

When you have everything, continue to stay modest.
If you lose it all and have nothing, remain patient until your time comes.
Be genuine during your ups, level headed during your downfalls.
Continue the same humility, when your life returns to normal.

You can lose something that you never really had
Existing beyond your means, counting eggs before they hatch.
Priorities over luxuries, misconstruing circumstances
Credibility and popularity shouldn't be the basis of you actions

* <u>If so, your priorities are mess up!!</u>
Getting financial advancements, excessive spending became a habit.
Debt stacked up to the ceiling, with no established line of credit.
Hustle for show money, when really you owe money.
Getting product on consignment but end up spending all of your earnings.

*<u>If so, your priorities are messed up!!</u>
Back to ground zero, burning bridges along the way.
Saturated with gasoline, combusting into flames
Slowly weakening the structure and every link along the way.

The Pen Is The Most Powerful Weapon

* if so, your priorities are all messed up!!!
Greed spreads like a diseased due to in consistencies
Priorities should supersede any wants when you have mouths to feed.
Running the streets with a stolen pistol and yet you have no felonies.
Riding like you're above the law, disregarding all legal formalities.

*If so your priorities are messed up!!
Switching lanes while counting change but priorities didn't change.
Still placing wants before needs until the law got in the way
An acquired taste for the finer things but can't accommodate the fees.
Having beer money but chasing champagne dreams

*If so your priorities are all messed up!!
Understanding right from wrong but still negative action
However, recognize that every actions reciprocates a reaction.
All for a social status when none of it really matters,
Obligations slowly turn into complicated situations.

Spiritual Warfare

How can you fight a battle you never knew existed?
A mind numbing experience, comparable to your soul suspended in remission.
Dancing with the devil while still rejecting his advancements

Pry away from his lies, broken promises, and deceptions
There are three sides of every story, based solely on individual perception.
Every now and then it's best to listen then to have to learn a lesson.

Passion for developing the truest potential without overcrowding and blessings.
Amid a positive approach instead of apprehensive comprehension.
A war's going on, innocent bystanders ensnared within the trenches.

The middle is by far, the worst possible position..
Torn between the two sides in spite of the bludgeon during depleted
One side has to triumph while the other is defeated.
Preparation and strategy is the key to any battle of the beasts,
Remembering the competitor was once an ally prior to removal off the team.

The Pen Is The Most Powerful Weapon

Those that pursue wealth become conscious that their efforts are insignificant.

Without the proper guidance only leads to ignorance Fools fold their hands and ravage themselves egoistically Better one handed with tranquility than a life full of misery.

Than two hands fill with toil chasing after the breeze
Certain experiences in your life are only forr your eyes to see.
What good is it for someone to gain the entire world?
Yet he has to forfeit and sacrifice his soul?

JyJuan Brock

Mind Race

Faded portraits hanging from a broken picture frame
Mirrors revealing images designed to manipulate the brain
Pages began to turn; picture started falling out of place
Tattered photo book, where memoirs took precedence of the space.

~~~

Panicked attempts to fight anxieties grasp, leaving self crippled with apprehension
A coed of three strands aren't easily broke; anger, depression.
Praying it's not hereditary trait that our children could inherit.
Being on the run from yourself, a lifetime watching through a rear view mirror.

~~~

Mind chasing can make an individual momentarily insane.
No one can completely comprehend, which make it difficult to understand.
Playing catch up with your thoughts, barely able to think straight.
A race within yourself, still finishing last place.

~~~

So cluttered completely running out of breathing space.
Thoughts scattered all over the making it tough to concentrate.
What's even harder is that not too many can relate?

The Pen Is The Most Powerful Weapon

Time to come up with a different option A means to escape

JyJuan Brock

On My Last Breath

On my last breath, I pray that made my momma proud
All the pain I put her through when I was a troubled child
Before, I go, I want to be able to make her smile.

On my last breath, I want to clear my slate of all my sins
With a fresh start and a new beginning, I didn't like where I was heading.

Life of destruction, had to edit scenes just to have a proper ending.
And to be a role model before my chances are depleted.

On my last breath, I want to complete my bucket list,
To be able to enjoy living and all of its offerings
Wanting my kids to experience everything in life I never did.

For once, being proud of myself foe all I accomplished
On my last breath, I want to leave behind a legacy.
Something for my kids to be proud of, and a way for them to remember me.

Explaining that knowledge equal power, studying is the key
With hard work and dedication you can achieve anything.

On my last breath, I want my brother and me to rebuild our rapport.
We started off as best friends, long before we knew what friends were.

The Pen Is The Most Powerful Weapon

Always had each other's back through every storm and any weather.

It didn't matter the size, some were small, and some were bigger.

If they fought on, they fought the both of us together.

JyJuan Brock

We Do Recover

Mechanisms in the human body allow for wounds to revitalize.
The same options don't apply for painful segments in our lives.
Those abrasions are undying scars that we attempt to disguise.
In due course, we will recover one day at a time.

What doesn't kill us, changes our performance and will to survive.
Facts force us to live in the truth without living a lie. You do what you have to, and not what you want to, to get where you need to be.
Psychological changes as the body start aging; still knowledge is the key.

Do not make an excuse to justify any of you actions.
What meant to be; was meant to be.
What will happen; was meant to happen. There
is no excuse but to execute.
For every action there's a reaction

Instead of doubts and worry over what we can't control,
Shift that energy to what we can.
First, create a goal, which is realistically, obtained.
Second, find the means to formulate a plan.
Third, situate what you collected, and execute your dreams.

The Pen Is The Most Powerful Weapon

Due to lack if ignorance, it's easier than it seems
If you believe in self, you can accomplish anything Do away with selfish habits; learn to work together as a team.

Surround yourself with those whom inspire, not people with any ill intent.
When you play an active role to find self security & self worth.
You will see the transformation in life, starting with self first.

JyJuan Brock

Freedom Isn't really Free

Life bestowed upon us is merely circumstantial evidence.
Of all life's oppressions given to us by the government
Impeding certain motives behind the draped curtain of politics.

Living on borrowed time, reality is the basis of experience
Searching for individuality while jeopardizing integrity on the obvious.
Ignorance of the law is no excuse for incompetence. The way the world revolves around treachery and acts of violence.

Freedom is never free; let not a soul tell you different.
Would you rather live free or live a life of the imprisoned?
The wealthy preserves their riches,
While those of misfortune scramble around for pennies.
Sacrifices to be made before understanding the distinction.

Death is the only things that's certain that separates us from the living.
Targets illustrated on our backs, slowly corned into submission.
Housed in concentration camps filled with men, woman and children.

Weakness isolated during interrogation of a witness
Those you thought were friends, are spectators in attendance

The Pen Is The Most Powerful Weapon

Firing squad using every piece of ammo that is given
We are prisoners of war, executed for acts of treason At what price de we really pay to live a life of freedom?

JyJuan Brock

Sinful Acts

Complicating our love by lusting over forbidden fruit
Curiosity makes us do things we mentally wouldn't do.
Altering the dynamics by having nothing left to lose
When Adam laid eyes on Eve, love branded him as a fool
Heart exposed to matures elements, left completely in the nude
Trying to capture Eve's affection by doing the unthinkable.

\ \ \ \ \

Either stupid or cockiness that goes against life's guiding principles.
When a fool falls in love he'll sacrifice independence for one that's less rationale.
Darkness can't drive out hate; that's something only love can prove.
By breaking the Garden of Eden's single solitary rule He pilfered the sacred apple disregarding all protocols.

\ \ \ \ \ \ \

Was a brazen act of valor, yet a foolish feat to execute?
Stimulating emotions rekindling the flame between the two
There is no right way to do the wrong thing, and expect different results.

Gotta know what's worth keeping and what is worth letting go.
The punishment for ignorance is a lifetime full of hurt We'll have to live with our decisions until we're six feet in the dirt.

The Pen Is The Most Powerful Weapon

``````

He sent down a loyal subject to help him figure out the truth.
The Goddess of Love carried satchel with her work-related tools.
He or she who owns the tools, has the ability to change the rules

And to unify two lonely souls while introducing them to the truth

```````

While standing beyond the alter rehearsing their sacred oath
Sanctified vowels of devotion, dedication, and love
Making them realize that such a brazen act was both chivalrous and dumb

The sacrifices people make for love can erratically compulsive as they come
Goes back to the old saying," that you lie and you learn".
Exchanging of their vowels while the goddess played her part

``````

"If you can't be supportive at their worst, you don't deserve them at their best".
Learn to be thankful for what you have, while pursuing true happiness
``````

JyJuan Brock

Through sickness and health, together through thick and thin
Have to move as a unit in order for you to win
Sometimes making the ultimate sacrifice for the benefit of the team
Love's essence is built off of compromise, and compatibility
```````

"You know you're in love when reality is better than your dreams."
What is pleasure in its simplest form?
It's the enjoyable feeling of satisfaction that you'll receive.
```````

The Pen Is The Most Powerful Weapon

Played Yourself Out Of Position

Bootlegging their own name all for social recognition
With a room full of tension, fools gathered in attendance
Some cut from a different cloth, real can recognize the realness.
Others stare at their own reflection disgusted by its appearance.

Moving as a single unit, wolves converge against the timid,
In a dog eat dog world, the weak is pushed out of position.
Head barely above water, revealing no hidden agendas
Air needed for survival but water's the basis of all existence
Mind is playing tricks, thoughts creating their own attentions.

Intentions create its own reality of what it is and what it isn't.
Trying to focus on what's right while making wrong decisions.
Filled with co-conspirators as well as co-dependents.

Still working to get ahead, but stuck in the off position
Consuming their souls with lies that carry over the deep end.
Judgement means that they view the world as it is, rather than what it isn't.

JyJuan Brock

Tempting to sell off a premonition to anyone who dares to listen.
One person's lie can pollute an entire village

A genocide that's so explicit, it burns down all enduring bridges.

No one left to save due to all the wrong provisions. One that doesn't tell a lie, has one less thought that needs remembered.
Lies breed more lies covered from your feet up to your knees in.
Bullshit that once said enough they slowly start to believe in.
When is enough really enough? You played yourself out of position!!!

The Pen Is The Most Powerful Weapon

Back Where It All Began

Back to where it all began, against all odds but still I stand
Questioned time and time again. On what's if takes to be attain.
Insanity was all that was said, without deviating form the plan.

The strategies remained the same, results in turn have never changed.
Puppets bound by yards of string, shackles, cuffs, bars, and chains.
Fragile strands on legs and hands. A hollowed shell, a lifeless frame.

Resurrected from a shallow grave, battered, bruised, stone, afraid.
As souls begins to fade away, who's left to take hold of the reigns
False since of hope for brighter days. Drag to my knees and pray for rain.

Tear drops fall onto the frame, to help to wash away the pain.
My life, my story, my pain, mu sins, it hands for most to comprehend.

A reflection of how to co-exist without judgement of peers and our close friends.

JyJuan Brock

Through freedom isn't really free, tragedy strikes in sets of threes.

The puppet master pulling strings, manipulating everything I think there for I am, writing helps escape reality. Panting a canvas of all of life's restraints, and all of life's possibilities.

The Pen Is The Most Powerful Weapon

Here and Now

Right now is all we have,
However, times are bound to get easier
Deferred by memories of the past
But the days will get brighter.

Walking into the unknown
The blind leading the blind.
I'm in way over my head
Following the beat of a different drummer.

Daring to be what I want to be Challenging
the limitation of life.
Watching as the sun begins to shine
Breaking through the clouds of darkness.

A gun without a barrel
Missing a crucial piece of its puzzle.
Psychological malfunction In the
absence of its muzzle.

Sinful reputations as well as self-humiliation
Relentless complications.
When it comes to trading places
100 beats a second, pulse continues racing.

Broken hearts cracked in half
Its shell as fragile as an egg.
Keep well protected against the young & reckless

JyJuan Brock

Or the pain will still remain.

Little Brother

Figure out which one of two evils
It is one who idolize or a person bred with envy?
When it's two of the same relation.

There shouldn't be any competing
Although we have our little secrets
We trust each other to keep them.

Once you treat them as your equal
Respect level decreases
Because they are your sibling.

They know your strengths and your weakness Penny
pinching. The system without drawing attention
Selfish with their attentions, manipulating positions.

Just because you love them
Doesn't mean you can't love them from a distance
And just because you're angry
Doesn't mean that you see them any different.

The Pen Is The Most Powerful Weapon

Unguided Youth

It's funny how people change up watching how easily best friends turned into strangers
Snakes in the grass without a condom is living dangerous
Like a disease, cold, cold blood coursing through the veins creating cancer

Thick as thieves still remembering how we came up
Committed to a lifestyle, while considered armed and dangerous

Both moving reckless, walking through life without no guidance
Nobody unwanted attention by all of the neighbors within the projects

From the cradle to the grave, God be so unforgiving one committed to the grave,
while the others stuck in prison.\Best friends but more like brothers, couldn't tell the different. Came from the same sandbox , on the same block, we became each others siblings.

Wish you can go back in time, and ask him for his forgiveness How could you heal a brother and ruin your only friendship?

JyJuan Brock

Broken Beyond Repair

Bandaging a broken heart
Helps for wounds to properly heal
By keeping out the infection
While nursing it back to health
Dropping a coin into a wishing well
Hoping to answer all of our prayers
Rain isn't meant to interrupt our lives
But just to wash away a couple of layers
When we pray, we prayed for brighter days
Sunshine helped to dry up all our tears
Finally finding inner happiness
In the midst of all our fears
True love will bring you inner peace
You've been searching for years
One thing about inner beauty
Is that it's wasn't concealed
~~~
But when you come across the perfect one
You'll know the love is real!!!
"Never make excuses of who you are"
Never apologize for who you are
Or what they make you out to be
Love self-enough to stand the truths
Hold strong to those beliefs
~~~
Idolizing the wrong individuals
Who send off false subliminal
Those of drug dealers and criminals
who drive in exotic vehicles

The Pen Is The Most Powerful Weapon

~~~

In decisions is pure torture
corrupting everything within reach
Decisions not up for negotiations
or what we force ourselves to believe

~~~~~

Living an unlived life
Is it all just make believe
No more tip toeing through nightmares
Because life is but a dream

JyJuan Brock

Circumstantial Misdirection

Having a friend that's intellectual seems to bring out the best in you....
Platonic and professional communications are acceptance skepticisms of relations that's anything less than sexual
Keeping it business casual work attire that stays professional.

Spending more time perfecting their looks than they do for their hearts.
Where we are in life can determine who we are? In the midst of sleep, God is there to do maintenance on your soul.
On the road to success, no short cuts you only reap what you saw.

Is our love premeditated or is it a crime of passion?
With emotional advancements not too many can imagine
Passive aggressive from the past while inhibiting the present....
The clock continues ticking every minute and every second
True love is unconditional not love with condition No placing stipulations and limits on how much love can be given.

But the love that we exhibit supersedes all superstition
True Love is selfless without any boundaries in existence
Most would love to give it but only if they had permission
Lust and Love racing neck always in competition

The Pen Is The Most Powerful Weapon

Hopefully, it's not too late to understand the difference.

JyJuan Brock

Product of Circumstance

Not a product of my environment, but a product of circumstance.
Through Federal Enhancements still believe in a second chance.
Too young to understand yet still forced to be a man
Reality stepping in hoping to only do 65%.

The first step is to act because ignorance is no excuse
Next step is to adapt to someone else's set of rules
Some have everything to gain and has nothing left to use
The blind leading the blind subject themselves to this abuse
Caught while selling crack even worse if a weapons present.

Now ask yourself this question, was the gun use for protection?
Or was it a tool used as an intimidation tactic?
Here is a difference in opinion, certain questions are never answered.
May have been a chemical imbalance but there is a consequence for every action...
Partial accountability and repercussions to process
On a one way trip prison because our circumstances got us

The Pen Is The Most Powerful Weapon

When Love Met Hate

When Love met Hate. They were both one in the same
In the pursuit of total happiness there was a thin line in between.
One heated might of passion could lead to lifetime full of pain.
Both parties pointing fingers but neither wants to take the blame.

Hurt People, Hurt people, that's why it's best to get to know people.
Whether it's his-story or her-story. Both parties born are created equal

Can make a song together but can't talk together so what's the lesser of the two evil? communication plays a major role. The lack of is kept a secret.

Love is love til' the two broke up now hatreds coursing through the veins.
From scorned hearts to malicious way to hide the fact that they're still in pain
Just know that once the damage is done things will never be the same.

Both were active participants in the sick and twisted game
We went from textbook educate depicting falsified images
Instead basic conversation communication via text messages.

JyJuan Brock

Personalities tend to change soon as you jump into a relationship
Shinning like a diamond but fake as a cubic zirconium
Leading us to ugly truth.
That there's three sides to every story.

One plaintiff one dependent and there's a judge without a jury.
With one coin comes two sides-right and right and wrong or love and hate.
Manipulation through conversation was the very first mistakes.

Dom Perion and fresh cherries as we eat by candle light
If loving you was wrong then its already too late Wedding dresses and ice cream with icing smeared across out face.
Compassion written across her face making the perfect candidate

During certain seasons in life it can get easy to forget To set our hearts to rest in the present while still healing from the past
Hatred stirs up conflicting issues unmasking certain elements of the game

Also expressing complete complete confidence. The reality of love regardless of the circumstances...
Had her and lost her. Thought that one would never love again
Broken Lost. Squandered, Stolen

Learning the definition of what's considered a romance

The Pen Is The Most Powerful Weapon

Lost soul left behind in hopes to become a man
Soul buried beneath the ashes and it rose back up again
Red Pill. Blue Pill. Poison or Potion

Hate written in bold letters and love is written in small captions
In a love /hate relationship there a slip side to every coin
Quickly distinguish the minor set backs so you know what to avoid

JyJuan Brock

The Race is Fixed

Just started the race, running in place to cross the finish line
Moving at moderate pace disregard the ones that's left behind

No matter what you do in life people will always criticize
Trapped in the middle off a thunder storm and there is nowhere left To hide...

When your back's against the wall and the wells completely dry
Who can you really trust with the pain and shame you feel inside?

Maybe its time to step and evaluate both sides
Being chased down by the consequences of wrong choices in our lives.

Rome wasn't build in one day. So take it one day at a time.
Calculate your moments and push the pride aside
Can't stay in the shell forever. The outside is just as nice.
Piecing the soul for your transgressions and crushed your heart for telling lies...

Through all the love, the hate, the passion, and pain that's seen through those two eyes...
Peace isn't determined by the present.
So it's time to spread those wings and fly....

The Pen Is The Most Powerful Weapon

Though you sat in total darkness. It's only because you closed your eyes

A helpless sheep without its shepherd is considered legally blind
Started running out of patience and slowly running out of time
The light at the end of the tunnel is what keeps the faith alive

All you'll ever need in this world of sin is just a nickel and a dime
Now place those both close together and see how bright they'll shining

JyJuan Brock

Now Take a Walk in My Shoes

Take a walk in my shoes
And you'll never make any commitments
The best way to keep your word is to try not to give in.

Take a walk in my shoes.
Where court is held in the trenches
Pistols are mandatory both playing offense and defense
Take a walk in my shoes.

You'll see things a lot differently
The weak are often weal because they chose to stay asleep.

Take a walk in my shoes
In the midst of pain and confusion
Plenty hidden distraction destined to mask what the truth is.

Take a walk in my shoes
While trying to escape reality
Not allowing your hustle determine the basis of your salary.

Take a walk in my shoes.
Experiencing exactly how I feels
To be hung by a judge and a jury of your peers.

Take a walk in my shoes
Out of mind out of sight
Everything that's done in the dark will show in daylight.

Take a walk in my shoes

The Pen Is The Most Powerful Weapon

Your mind needing time to Re-group where
some prefer a beautiful lie to an ugly truth.

Take a walk in my shoes
And getting thrown over the deep end
Not to see if we could swim but to punish us for our sins.

Take a walk in my shoes
Realizing that drug money's just a short term loan
That you end up paying back in lawyers or jail time

Take a walk in my shoes
Becoming a target of our environment
Bullseye painted across the chest so police have a target to fire at

Take a walk in my shoes
You'll know to always keep the grass low
So when they slither through your lawn the snakes head eventually Shows....

Take a walk in my shoes
Stain your lane play your position
Life is about growth. Transformation and minding your own business.

Take a walk in my shoes
Very rarely would you see me smile
Pops wasn't around so mamma had to hold it down

Take a walk in my shoes

JyJuan Brock

There wouldn't be too much comparing
Now my pain is your pain and my spirit is your spirit
Take a walk in my shoes

Seeing your back against the ropes
With nobody else to turn to not even flesh and blood.

Take a walk in my shoes
Carrying that monkey on your shoulders
With an addiction to the life style,
The money and the power.

Take a walk in my shoes
On the side line no one to cheer you on
Determined to finish the race though in the middle of a thunderstorm
Now take a walk in my shoes.

The Pen Is The Most Powerful Weapon

To My Son

To my son such a remarkable young man, full of intelligence, purpose, and I'm so proud to call you my son. God has a way to turn a bad situation into something promising for your future.

To my son, my first born, while editing your second book, your writing has inspired me to tell my story.

To my son, there were many time that I was the student and you were the teacher.

To my son I have learned so much through your strength about myself that the apple don't fall to far the tree.

To my son I can honestly say I'm proud of you and your brother. How God has molded the both of you to be strong men with a purpose.

To my son, remember once you take accountability of your wrongs, God will do the rest.

To my son your story will always give you glory and every test is a testimony.

To my son when things seemed to be falling apart it's really coming together.

JyJuan Brock

To my son God only uses the best to carry out his mission. To my son continue to shine and continue to soar like an eagle.

Love you so much
From Mom

The Pen Is The Most Powerful Weapon

Synophois

My writings started off as just a hobby, a mean for an escape. As a direct result, I learned that in writing, you have the freedom of self-expression and free reign on using your creativity. Some individuals just aren't good at verbally expressing themselves. Without an outlet, those suppressed feelings emotions usually fester until it reaches its breaking point, typically leading to catastrophic conseguences.

By writing, the pen and pad became my personal canvas, my voice of reasoning, and my outlet. In my eyes, my writings became a form of therapy allowing myself to have a release without criticism for being different. Once my pen hits the paper, it begins to have a mind of its own, flowing freely without any care in the world. This allowed me to creatively close certain chapters of my life while encompassing the specific reasons for my detrimental outlook on those issues. That is when I realized that I actually half a talent I didn't even know I had and that I was far more intelligent than I led myself to believe.
The pen truly is mightier than the sword.

JyJuan Brock

The Pen Is The Most Powerful Weapon

JyJuan Brock